INTENTIONAL COMMUNITIES
HOW TO START THEM & WHY

INTENTIONAL COMMUNITIES
HOW TO START THEM & WHY

J. Donald Walters

Crystal Clarity, Publishers
14618 Tyler Foote Road
Nevada City, CA 95959

Cover design by Bella Potapovskaya

Copyright © 1968 by
Swami Kriyananda

Second edition, 1968
Third edition, 1969
Fourth edition, 1970
Fifth edition, 1970
Sixth edition, 1971
Seventh edition 1972
Eighth edition, 1979
Ninth edition, revised and updated, 1988, by
    J. Donald Walters
Tenth edition, 1990

(J. Donald Walters has written various books under the name Swami Kriyananda.)

Previously named Cooperative Communities — How to Start Them, and Why

All Rights Reserved
International Book Number 0-916124-20-7
Printed in the United States of America

Dedication

This book is lovingly dedicated to my spiritual teacher, Paramhansa Yogananada, who envisioned "world brotherhood colonies" as one of the solutions to the problems nowadays besetting mankind.

Other books by the same author:

Cities of Light
Education for Life
The Art of Supportive Leadership
The Path
Crises In Modern Thought
Rays of the Same Light
The Land of Golden Sunshine
The Artist as a Channel
Affirmations & Prayers
Secrets of Happiness
Secrets of Success
Secrets of Attracting and Keeping Friends
Secrets of Persuasion
Secrets of Meditation
Secrets of Inner Peace
Secrets of Overcoming Harmful Emotions
The Story of Crystal Hermitage

Contents

Introduction to the 1988 Edition 9
1. The Time is Now 15
2. Self-Realization vs.
       The Megalopolis 20
3. Intentional Communities and
       The Quest for Opportunity ..28
4. Intentional Communities,
       Past and Present 40
5. How to Begin 51
6. Communal Economics 69
7. Communalism vs. Privacy 80
8. Education 90
9. Government 100
10. Rules 110
11. What is Ananda? 115

Introduction to the 1988 Edition

I first wrote and published this little book in 1968. My purpose at that time was twofold: to suggest general guidelines for people interested in communities; and to offer a blueprint for an intentional community that I myself wanted to found. My hope was to enlist a number of friends in this venture.

Since that time, both of those purposes have been realized. The community I envisioned got off to a good start, and continues to flourish, with a very low rate of attrition. And this booklet remains, after more than two decades,

Intentional Communities

---

the manual most looked to by people interested in starting communities of their own.

The present edition has been extensively revised and updated to correspond to the fruits of experience. Early suggestions that later proved impracticable have been abandoned, or else adjusted to correspond to reality. Other suggestions, based on living experience, have been added. Thus, this booklet is as universally practical as I am able to make it.

Nearly thirty years of research went into the first preparation of this handbook. My thrust, during that preparatory period, was never romantic or academic. It was always to provide workable guidelines. I enjoyed reading "utopian" novels about idyllic societies, as much, probably, as anyone. My concern, however, was never with beautiful but impractical theories. It was with concepts that stood a chance of being actu-

Introduction to the 1988 Edition

ally realized on the hard ground of this world.

I first became interested in intentional communities when I was fifteen. World War II was raging at that time. America, following the disaster of Pearl Harbor, had just entered the conflict. Perhaps it was the hatred and suffering generated by war that helped push me in the direction of seeking an alternative to the arrogant self-affirmation and selfish nationalism that was the spur to that conflict. To me, even then, the thought of people of basically similar interests living in community, and sharing together the struggles of life, offered the best possible answer to some of the pressing problems of our times, relating to the search for human and spiritual values in a seemingly purposeless universe.

For many years thereafter I fairly devoured every book I could find on communities, past and present. When-

Intentional Communities

ever I could, I visited functioning communities. One such was Dayalbagh, near Agra in India. Another was a kibbutz, near Galilee in Israel. I also visited and studied, from a communitarian point of view, numerous monastic communities throughout the world.

I spoke and corresponded, as well, with a number of people whose expertise might offer solutions to some of the practical problems I anticipated in the founding of a workable community. Among these people was Jayprakash Narayan, formerly the number two man in India after Jawaharlal Nehru. Jayprakash Narayan had left government service in the hope of finding communitarian solutions to India's problems. He was gracious enough to express enthusiasm for my ideas.

My adult work of many years as an organizer, administrator, teacher, and counselor provided me with direct, practical experience in the intricacies of

Introduction to the 1988 Edition

group dynamics.

My enthusiasm for this project received special impetus when, in 1948, I met the great master Paramhansa Yogananda, and was accepted by him as a disciple. For I soon learned that the communitarian ideal was dear to him also.

One of the basic aims of Yogananda's mission to the West was thus stated by him: "To spread a spirit of brotherhood among all peoples, and to aid in establishing, in many countries, self-sustaining world brotherhood colonies for plain living and high thinking."

For years as his disciple I studied everything he had said to me and others, and everything he had written, on this subject.

The first edition of this book was instrumental in the founding of Ananda World Brotherhood Village, in the Sierra Nevada foothills of northern California. Ananda has since become recognized as

Intentional Communities

one of the most successful intentional communities in the world. Numbering several hundred residents, it has branch communities in various parts of America, and one also near Assisi, Italy.

Roughly half a century, then, has gone into the study and planning of this booklet, and into the testing of its principles and practices. I need hardly add that I believe deeply in the principles outlined here. I have lived them in one form or another for most of my adult life. If, through this manual, I succeed in convincing even a few people to live similarly, I shall feel my life's labor to have been richly rewarded.

Chapter One

The Time is Now

In his last years on earth, the great teacher Paramhansa Yogananda repeatedly and urgently spoke of a plan that he said was destined to become a basic social pattern for the new age: the formation of "world brotherhood colonies," as he called them. In almost every public lecture, no matter what his announced subject, he would digress to urge people to act upon his proposal.

"The day will come," he predicted, "when this idea will spread through the world like wildfire. Gather together,

Intentional Communities

those of you who share high ideals. Pool your resources. Buy land in the country. A simple life will bring you inner freedom. Harmony with nature will give you a happiness known to few city dwellers. In the company of other truth seekers it will be easier for you to meditate and to think of God.

"What is the need for all the luxury with which people surround themselves? Most of what they have they are paying for on the installment plan. Their debts are a source of unending worry to them. Even people whose luxuries have been paid for are not free. Attachment makes them slaves. They consider themselves freer for their possessions, and don't see how their possessions in turn have possessed them!"

Yogananda stressed the joys of simple, natural living and God thinking — a way of life that, he said, would bring people "happiness and freedom." But his message went beyond simply

The Time is Now

presenting people with an attractive idea. There was also urgency in his plea.

"The time is short," he repeatedly told his audiences. "You have no idea of the sufferings that await mankind. In addition to wars there will be a depression the like of which has not been known in a very long time. Money will not be worth the paper it is printed on. Millions will die."

On one occasion he cried: "You don't know what a terrible cataclysm is coming!"

To place reliance upon prophetic utterances may strike some people as superstitious. Even these people, however, may be interested to note that, of persons reputed to have prophetic vision, every single one has predicted terrible sufferings for humanity in the years to come.*

But it is not necessary to rely blindly

---

*Bhrigu, an Indian sage, wrote: "There will be weeping in every home."

Intentional Communities

on prophecies. The events they have predicted are already too visibly probable.

Numerous scientists have predicted, on the basis of known facts, that the present population explosion can have only one result: In the years to come "hundreds of millions" of people in the world must either die of starvation, for lack of sufficient food on our planet to feed them, or be destroyed in a holocaust as they struggle for whatever food they can get. Economic depression of massive proportions has been predicted by reputable economists. And as for warfare, one must, of course, always hope for the best — but what real chances are there, think you, for a cessation of conflict? The pressures continue to mount. They have not lessened, even with the threat of global destruction.

Let us consider the solution that Yogananda proposed — that of "world brotherhood colonies" — or intentional communities, to use a term that is better known. It was, to be sure, a solution for the individual, not a universal solution that he was stressing. Yet many universal changes have proceeded from the personal transformation of individuals. (Witness the widespread upliftment that grew out of the teachings of Buddha and Jesus Christ. The ensuing social revolutions were out of all proportion to the few disciples converted by those great masters.)

There is, moreover, at this time in history, an implication in this idea of intentional communities that lifts it quite out of the personal category, into something sociological and universal.

Chapter Two

Self-Realization vs. The Megalopolis

No one needs a sociologist to tell him that the trend of this twentieth century is toward consolidation. Small businesses, unable to compete with the large corporations, become swallowed up by them. Large corporations, again, merge with others, in time to become vast industrial empires.

Societies of men are moving inexorably toward a centralization of power. The world's increasing population necessitates increasing government con-

Self-Realization vs. The Megalopolis

trol. The old argument between states' rights and federal rights is an anachronism. It is impossible nowadays, legislatively and economically, to return the power to local governments. Instead, the trend is toward the consolidation not only of cities and states, but of countries.

What will the result of this process be for man, the individual?

It is in the interests of economy and efficiency that groups of people unite. The danger, however, is that those same principles, economy and efficiency, will demand of people a uniformity that extends to their personal lives as well. Numerous social thinkers have noted that individual tastes and values, too, must be, and are being, increasingly subordinated to the institutional order — the "Establishment."

To the institutional mind, such uniformity may seem an end and a blessing in itself. Selfish individualism is decried by such people, and of course, when defined as selfish, rightly so. But consoli-

Intentional Communities

dation is posed by them as the only alternative, and anyone supporting such a trend is hailed as a "liberal."

Is it truly liberal to destroy human liberty? Voluntary cooperation is one thing; enforced uniformity, quite another.

There is a third alternative open to man. *It lies in a recognition of the fact that the mainspring of mature action is the inner man, not an outer order.*

To imagine that systems can be anything more than a convenience has been man's mistake. Systems are not an end in themselves. They cannot inspire men to perfection. At best, they may prevent a few people from behaving too outrageously.

The more society becomes centralized in its power, the greater the need for individuals to seek their values (as opposed to their outer convenience) *within themselves.* For man is more than a cog in the social wheel. The systems he

Self-Realization vs. The Megalopolis

adopts are supposed in some way to benefit *him*, individually, and not merely to serve the good of some separate entity, unrelated to any of its members, called "society." To speak of society, as some writers have done, as an "organism," is misleading. From *within* ourselves come our inspiration, our understanding, our love and happiness. All that we experience outside ourselves depends upon our inner *capacity* for experience. Man is a *source* of light, not a mirror.

Thus, the point must come in modern social evolution when men, instead of submitting placidly to the outward demand for uniformity, rise up individually to reassert their worth as human beings.

The trend of which we speak is inevitable. Offsetting the push to uniformity, in fact, the modern era has seen a rising tide of insistence on the dignity of the individual. In communistic countries

Intentional Communities

the governments have tried to curb this tendency, yet even there it is clearly in evidence.

It was even in evidence in the utterly dehumanizing atmosphere of the World War II concentration camps. There, too, individuals could be found who, in their resistance to the sordid influences around them, rose like lotuses from the mud and blossomed to greatness.

It is time to press forward from a preoccupation with outward systems to a recognition of the real key to the efficacy of any system: individual man. The need of the hour is for self-unfoldment — not as a selfish imposition on the universe (the "Great God, *Ego*" of Ayn Rand) — but simply as a private and deeply personal search for Self-realization.

The result cannot but benefit man in his political, economic, and social institutions as well. For life is harmonious outwardly when men have inner har-

Self-Realization vs. The Megalopolis

mony. And nothing brings outward harmony when men live inwardly in disharmony.

The question arises: How, without imposing on anyone else, may one develop inner clarity in the midst of social confusion? It is difficult to have inner peace when one is surrounded by chaos. It is difficult to progress steadily in one direction through swirling currents that seek to draw one off in a million other directions.

Consider: What need is there to cling to city life? If it doesn't happen to suit one, what moral end can be served by sticking grimly to it? The chance that somehow it may be molded in time to become a universal blessing? It is not his systems that bless man, but man who blesses his systems by having the good will to make them work.

No, it is not necessary from any standpoint — social, philosophical, personal — to remain in an environment

Intentional Communities

that is not conducive to one's welfare. For the man of aspiring mind, the megalopolis of modern times ceases to be even the convenience that so many people find it. Instead, it becomes an obstruction. He must find his way, just as soon as circumstances allow him to do so, to the sanity and peace of a simpler way of life.

A person who devotes himself to the development of an inner awareness is in a vastly better position than one who, his very self-respect assaulted by competing hordes, has all he can do to maintain a little sense of his own identity.

One reads with horror newspaper accounts of people who watched calmly, refusing to become involved, as some major crime was committed, or as someone fell and died in the street. It would seem that the average city dweller's technique for preserving his own sanity is to isolate himself from the world around him, and from his fellow man.

Self-Realization vs. The Megalopolis

Stranded and alone on the tiny island of his ego, is it any wonder that he complains of feeling alienated?

"This above all," Shakespeare wrote, "to thine own self be true, and it must follow, as the night the day, thou canst not then be false to any man."

Without self-respect, how can there be a proper respect for others? Without self-awareness, how can there be a sensitivity to the needs of others? The wellsprings of charity must flow from the inner man. They cannot reach him by a process of invasion.

To "hie away" to the country, then, need in no way imply a rejection of one's social responsibilities. It can become, rather, the beginning of a sincere assumption of responsibility, not only for oneself, but, by extension, toward society at large.

Chapter Three

Intentional Communities and the Quest for Opportunity

Why do people move to the city? The main reasons are easy to find. In cities, jobs are more plentiful, social life is more varied, cultural stimuli are incomparably greater than in rural areas.

Country living, by contrast, whatever its natural appeal, poses severe disadvantages for the average person. Economic opportunities are relatively few. Most people are not farmers even by in-

The Quest for Opportunity

clination. Their skills are city skills: those of the merchant who needs customers for his wares; of the secretary who can work only if there are letters to type; of the teacher who needs students to teach. Any move on one's own to the country would require total reeducation, and perhaps, for all that, a life of relative uselessness.

And what of social opportunities? If a person has no inclination for farming, he is not likely to want to spend his leisure time hobnobbing with people whose chief interests center on the state of the season's crops.

What comes with difficulty on one's own, however, is accomplished with relative ease in a group. Persons of like interest, banding together in communities, preserving their customary interdependence, each contributing his own skills to the whole — under such circumstances, there is no reason why the city person need feel out of place.

Intentional Communities

Consider, in this context, the simple question of artistic and intellectual opportunities.

In variety, small communities cannot compete with the cities. The greatest satisfaction in the arts, however, lies in creating, not merely in being entertained. In this area of life, the intentional community could offer incomparably more than the big city: the time to create, an interested audience, inspiring natural surroundings, and an opportunity to explore and develop one's inner life.

Nor need a variety of stimulation be lacking. A community accustomed to good libraries would find sufficient incentive to create at least an adequate library of its own. Outside lecturers could be invited to come and speak. An occasional outing to the city to attend a symphony concert or an art exhibit would afford as much cultural exposure as most city dwellers ever get.

There is no earthly reason why a

The Quest for Opportunity

community seeking a more natural way of life should utterly reject the benefits of modern civilization. Perfect isolation would be economically unsound, even if it were in some way desirable. Unless one wanted to revert to some sort of Neanderthal existence, complete self-sufficiency would mean that a community would have to produce, at enormous expense, all of its own machinery, its plumbing fixtures, its cooking and eating utensils, its clothing fabrics, even its own toothpaste. Considering how inexpensive such items are in our society, because produced on a mass scale, it seems only practical for a community to devote itself to selling what it can on the outside, and to buying what it needs with the profit.

The community might, in short, be similar in many ways to any village, with the basic distinction that it would be an *intentional* community. It would be based on cooperation, not competi-

Intentional Communities

tion, and on self-unfoldment rather than on self-aggrandizement at the expense of one's fellow beings.

Basic to the success of any community is the question of income. People living together cooperatively in the country could grow their own food, build their own buildings, perhaps make their own clothes. Many of the materials even for these basic necessities, however, would have to be brought in from outside. They would need an income with which to buy them.

What possible sources of income would there be for a community that lived well outside the busy industrial centers? The problem is less difficult than it may seem.

Presumably, persons coming to live in the community would bring with them certain skills, for some of which a ready market could be found in the nearby towns and cities. The skills might include handicrafts — wood carving, painting, weaving, sandal-making, pottery. More likely, they would involve practical trades, such as building and carpentry, and white collar skills such as typing, merchandising, and teaching. Because few persons are equipped with skills that would assist survival in the remote wilderness, and because most of those with a yen to hie away to distant mountain ranges are probably temperamentally unsuited anyway to living communally, it seems wise to consider buying land not very far from the mainstream of civilization.

Specialization is the hallmark of our age. It should not be difficult for creative minds to find some sort of industry in which the community could specialize, offering its product at a competitive price to the industrial, building, or mercantile world. This industry could even be sophisticated — the manufacture, for example, of electronic devices.

Books could be published, clothing

Intentional Communities

made, records produced, a mail order business developed. All of these could bring income to the community.

A major source of income could be weekend programs and seminars for outsiders.

Another possible source of income, and something that would be necessary in any case, would be a school for children. A school run on creative and idealistic lines should attract students from outside the community.

The community could also create its own dramas, pageants, and other artistic and spiritual entertainments, which it could offer to clubs, schools, and colleges around the country.

There is no reason why the community could not also open its own shops in larger communities nearby. These shops could serve also as outlets for community products.

Basic to the economic success of an intentional community would be the

The Quest for Opportunity

principle of cooperation. In the big cities, every man is obliged to compete for his place in the sun. Out of a thousand people, each has, potentially, 999 rivals. Anxiety, tension, frustration — such are a few of the known side effects. But consider also how much time and energy are devoted in ordinary business to out-maneuvering, outbidding, and out-shouting the other fellow, and how much money is spent for the ungenerous purpose of drawing shoppers away from his door to one's own.

Much has been written about the benefits of a competitive system. Certainly, the huge socialistic monopoly that is normally posed as an alternative, while it may result in less material waste, affords also less human incentive. But what of the small intentional community, where *voluntary cooperation* is taught as an alternative to both competition and monopoly?

Supposing that out of a thousand

Intentional Communities

people, each person had, not 999 rivals, but as many potential friends and colleagues? There is no reason why this should not be possible in a community that emphasized cooperation as a way of life. Does this sound like an "impossible dream"? Ananda Village is now old enough to claim to have withstood the test of time. The harmony within this community of several hundred members, and also with those outside the community with whom we deal, is legendary. So also is the level of prosperity legendary among experimental communities. Assuredly, cooperation is no merely utopian dream.

A number of intentional communities in the past, also, demonstrated considerable financial stability. Where they failed, the fault was due largely to an impractical effort to isolate themselves, or to too idealistic an expectation of human nature.

Cooperation, however, rightly

The Quest for Opportunity

understood, ought not by any means to be limited to the community. It should reach out to embrace the larger "community" of mankind. Hence, of course, Yogananda's term, "world brotherhood colony."

In India, the devout Hindu is taught, before eating a meal, to pour a libation of gratitude onto the ground from which the food has come; to give food to an animal, since it is with the help of animals that man obtains food; and to feed some hungry stranger whose position, but for his own good fortune, he might himself be sharing. Side by side, similarly, with a search for personal and communal prosperity, there should develop a sense of responsibility to society at large, without the existence of which the community would very likely be little more than a primitive tribe.

Instead of competition with the outside world, there should develop a sense of sharing with it. One important contri-

Intentional Communities

bution might be that of example.

Two donkeys were harnessed by a peasant to move a rock. But the animals pulled in opposite directions. Although they worked themselves to exhaustion, the rock was not moved an inch. What of a community where men have learned to act in a spirit of cooperation, not of ceaseless competition — where a little labor suffices to feed many mouths? Would such an example be totally lost on society at large?

Rome and Carthage, fighting each other to their mutual destruction, set an example for the ages of the uselessness of selfish greed. Better than ten negative examples, however, is one positive solution. What of a community that views others, not as competitors, nor as strangers, but as friends? Such a community, even if removed from the vortices of civilization, could be a more forceful influence for good than a dozen institutions that are more "involved," but also more submerged, in urban insanities.

Chapter Four

Intentional Communities, Past and Present

A remark that one often hears with respect to cooperative communities is, "So many have been started, but all of them have failed." This statement is simply not true. Actually, there have been a number of spectacular successes.

The Inspirationists of Amana, the Harmonists at Economy, the Mennonites, the Shakers, the Hutterites — these names are well known to history. They were wealthy. Some of them are still flourishing. That others eventually died

Intentional Communities, Past and Present

out — often after decades, or even after one or two centuries — need no more be termed a failure than the fact that almost all business concerns eventually die defines them as failures. The way of life is ever to grow, and then die. Without eventual death, room would never be made for new forms of life. Any institution that endures through the ages, indeed, is probably only a shell of its former self. At some point in its history, instead of dying, it must have chosen to become petrified.

In our own age we have only to look at the kibbutzim of modern Israel to see a movement that, for all its ups and downs, cannot in any way be termed a failure.

And there are the monasteries, similar in many ways, if not in all, to the intentional communities being considered here. Indeed, what community could be more intentional than a monastery?

It would be wise to consider briefly

various communal experiments, and to study the reasons why some of them failed, while others succeeded.

Often, as we have already said, the unsuccessful experiments were founded on too idealistic a view of human nature. A reading of *Kibbutz*, by Melford E. Spiro, conveys the impression that even the modern kibbutzim, while in themselves a decided success, have proved disillusioning to some of their members, who expected their way of life to evolve the "perfect" man. Rousseau's concept of "the noble savage" reads well in print, but one encounters this wonderful creature all too rarely here on ignoble earth. The jungle savage is often, in fact, *less* noble than his city counterpart. The belief that a return to nature will automatically produce good people is naive. The ensuing disappointment can well prove shattering.

Linked to too idealistic a view of human nature was the failure of commu-

Intentional Communities, Past and Present

nities — devastating to any but the best established — to screen their applicants. Robert Owen, in founding a utopian community at New Harmony, ~~Pennsylvania~~ [Indiana], did not take into account the danger of mixing people of diverse convictions. His community lasted only three years.

Perhaps one of the greatest mistakes that community planners made was to attempt too much with their plans. No system can create virtue. The most it can do is facilitate the development of virtue. For virtue is a development that must always spring from the good will of the individual members. "Freeland," a community founded in the 1890's on the basis of a book by the Austrian economist, Theodor Hertzka, failed largely for this reason. In trying to adhere too closely to Hertzka's elaborate blueprint, the community finally foundered in disillusionment.

A common failing of new communi-

Intentional Communities

ties has been the tendency to demand too radical a change of their members. In biology there is an axiom that evolution never moves by sudden leaps. This is certainly true, with very rare exceptions, of human nature. Leniency must be granted people, within reason, to grow at their own rate of speed.

Another defect in certain communal experiments has been a tendency to isolationism. A group of people that seek to cut off all ties with the outside world will find themselves forced to work tirelessly simply to produce the bare necessities. The first generation may be inspired, in reaction against modern life, to withdraw to such extremes. But unless their children are kept exceedingly uninformed, the chances are that when they grow up they will want to return to the cities, where at least one does not have to slave like a beast of burden merely to remain alive.

The consensus of persons who have

Intentional Communities, Past and Present

made a study of community life is that some definite communal structure is needed. Coupled to this advice, one always finds mentioned the need for strong leadership. People who are left to drift their own ways soon drift apart. A chicken with its head chopped off will run about erratically. A typical example of the problems encountered by societies that are ruled too rigidly by consensus was the unfortunate Icarian community, whose president was not free even to buy a sack of wheat without the specific consent of the whole community. Even people with the best of intentions require coordination in a group endeavor. The best that can come of rigid rule by consensus is an uninspired community in which every inching step forward is applauded as a giant leap.

Communities that have failed have done so, finally, because they lacked a clearly defined sense of purpose. A mere wish for economic stability does not seem to have been enough of a motive to inspire people to remain united. It is no accident that, of the successful ventures, nearly all have been spiritually inspired.

How, then, might the pitfalls we have outlined be avoided?

First, one should not expect miracles. It is enough if a new way of life be better than the old one. It is too much to ask that it also be perfect.

Policies pertaining to the acceptance of applicants are necessary. One carping faultfinder in a community can undermine the morale of many well-intentioned members. It would be wise, especially in a new community, to take care that only harmonious persons be admitted.

Again, there should be some system, some rule, though not with a view to creating goodness in people. The vital concern should be for people as individuals, and not as parts of a system.

Intentional Communities, Past and Present

Some sort of system will be needed only to coordinate the life of the community, not to be its salvation.

People should not be expected to embrace a way of life that is too radically different from the one to which they are presently accustomed. This caution is important especially from the standpoint of enforcing "togetherness." A community of like minds cannot be forged on the strength of any mere theory. People must grow to a sense of unity naturally. The safest course for a new community, especially, would be to allow each person the freedom to meet others on his own terms.

Finally, for a community to be intentional there must be *some* sort of leadership. Emerson wrote, "An institution is the lengthened shadow of one man." Such, throughout history, has nearly always been the case. A leader, however, is not a dictator. He encourages initiative on the part of others. He

Intentional Communities

places human values ahead of any system, and inspires people towards their own self-unfoldment.

The less tight-knit a community, the greater the chances of its having this type of a leader. Where people are expected to do everything in common, however, and to be of one mind on every issue, frictions can mount quickly. A community that strives for constant, intense "togetherness" will require miracles of leadership to survive.

Consider, then, another type of community: the normal village, where "togetherness" is not driven down people's throats. There, administration is easily kept to a minimum. Villages have endured, where close-knit intentional communities, lacking in strong leadership, have disintegrated.

The obvious solution, for those who do not favor a dictatorship, is simply not to demand from people a constant togetherness, and hence a measure of unanimity, for which they are unprepared. The leadership of a community might then be strong, but not fussy. People would be given the freedom to grow, but at the same time would be given enough of a sense of common direction to help them to grow together, not apart.

A safe beginning, surely, would be to heed well the fact that nearly all successful colonies have been spiritually oriented. If the idea of "world brotherhood colonies" is to spread, it would be well for at least the initial experiments not to be planned without including this (so far) all-but-essential ingredient.

A religious orientation, however, need not imply sectarianism. The essence of religion is its emphasis on an *inner* life. It is not because of religious fanaticism that communities have held together, but because the inner life developed in their members, through their faith, has given them the peace of mind to smile away petty annoyances, the

Intentional Communities

flexibility to meet others part way on disagreements, and the freedom to enjoy things without attachment. In the matter of emphasizing an inner life, no community can afford to be lax, even if its goals are not otherwise spiritual. It is to make an inner life possible that intentional communities are needed in the first place.

Chapter Five

How to Begin

I read once in a newspaper about someone who had been trying to start an ideal community, complete with progressive university, laboratories, concert halls — all the social amenities, in short, styled in impeccable architectural taste. He was trying to raise two and a half billion dollars for this dream-venture. Needless to say, the dream never materialized. Two and one-half billion dollars is hardly a pittance! Anyone with such an impractical scheme would be lucky to raise two and a half thousand. No one

Intentional Communities

wants to sail his money on the North Wind.

This example is worthy of notice, however. For people too often imagine that huge sums will be necessary for a worthy project to be launched, and before people can be brought together to work on it. This is true, no doubt, for some ventures — Disneyland, for example, which couldn't have been started without a huge initial investment. For intentional communities, however, the very opposite is true. People, by working together, *produce* wealth. Many great ventures, indeed, have started on a shoestring. Nor did Walt Disney himself start out in the world with the money to finance his future success.

Often, it is better to make a beginning with little than to spend years waiting for the skies to rain gold.

Others I have heard of, wealthy men, bought land with the intention of developing it for the future enjoyment of

How to Begin

many people. Theirs were charitable ventures, from which others were expected to benefit with a minimum of responsibility on the part of the members.

These men were at least in a position to build. But the willingness of people to accept their patronage, without assuming personal responsibility for the success or failure of the project, would spell sure death to any community. Even if people did work under such a scheme, what would their motive be? Gratitude? There is a point beyond which gratitude can become another word for slavery.

No, it is better for people to own their own venture, and to work for it secure in the knowledge that by so doing they are working for themselves.

One way to get started would be for interested persons to save toward the initial costs. It is not all that difficult nowadays for people to save up for things they really want. A hundred people each saving $1,000 would have

Intentional Communities

$100,000 — enough to make a very good beginning.

There are ways to make it easier to convert good intentions into reality. Consider this suggestion: Institute a "crash program" for several months. People can save considerably more than usual if they adopt the cooperative principle from the start, pooling their resources. Young people, especially, would find it easy to adapt themselves to such a scheme.

They could share their meals in common. The diet, during this period, might be simplified. Cooking for many would greatly reduce costs and labor. A set fee could be paid by each participant for expenses. Cooking could either be done by rotation on a voluntary basis, or paid for, the cooks raising their own $1,000 through their work in the kitchen. Whatever money is left over from the expense account could be used to buy grain for later use by the community.

How to Begin

Housing accommodations could be shared temporarily. To share one's room or apartment with others may not appeal to some people, but for a limited period of time it needn't prove a great hardship for people whose ideal is to live in community.

If this plan were not adopted, a regular weekly or monthly payment towards membership in the cooperative might ensure a more rapid saving than hoarding the money oneself against the day when this sum reaches the predetermined figure. ($300 in the bank, and a Sears Roebuck catalog by one's bed, can perform magic vanishing acts!)

The above suggestions, while reasonable enough in theory, demand a degree of faith, a firmness of purpose, and a clarity of vision that one rarely, if ever, encounters in large groups of people. Many people will get behind a venture once it has proved successful. Few, however, are visionary enough to dedi-

Intentional Communities

cate themselves with indomitable energy to a dream, especially to one for which there are not as yet many successful models. Ironically, while it takes manpower to make a communitarian dream successful, few people will join a communitarian venture until they see it already well on the road to success.

The more developed a venture of this type becomes, however, the greater the numbers of people who will get behind it. It seems wisest, therefore, to get the project "off the ground" as soon as possible, even with one broken wing, than to wait, discuss endlessly, and plan toward the Perfect Day.

If it is difficult to get large groups of people behind a reasonable plan for success, it is, unfortunately, even more difficult to persuade groups to back a "broken wing" type of beginning. Thus, it may prove necessary for a new community to be launched by a bare handful of individuals, inspired, perhaps, by only

How to Begin

one person with the dream and the determination to get the project "off the ground" despite every caution by the worldly wise that the thing simply can't be done.

In this case, the secret will lie in involving people stage by stage. Where they might be frightened off by the sheer magnitude of the project, were it presented to them as the creation of a thriving intentional village, it may prove relatively easy to invite their cooperation in constructing a less ambitious project — a place, say, for retreat, or for summer camping. The village itself could develop stage by stage, from a summer camp or a place of occasional retreat to a place with a small permanent staff, and so on, each step being taken as people feel ready for it.

In founding Ananda Village, I had to earn most of the initial money, and much of it for several subsequent years, myself. One really has no call to com-

Intentional Communities

plain if, in trying to do something for others, he finds their help somewhat elusive until the project is already off to a good start.

At first, many people evidently thought I wanted to take advantage of them. I remember my first venture at earning money for the project. I put out a record album of songs, hoping it would help finance the first step I envisioned toward the community: the building of a meditation retreat.

"So you can make lots of *money*, eh?" leered a popular talk show host on whose program I appeared, hoping to promote the album.

The first meeting I called of possibly interested people to discuss the project dissolved in accusations of suspected bad faith on my part.

The only way to proceed proved to be to take all the initial risks myself, while gradually involving more and more people in different aspects of the project as we went along, so they would not feel it was *my* project, but theirs. This, I feel, was important. It would never have done for me to do all the work for them. Group *involvement* is necessary in any group undertaking.

I remember an experience I had as a child. I'd been given a bicycle for my birthday. I was so happy to get this present that I spent most of my birthday party teaching the other children to ride. What I did was hold the bicycle by the seat and the handlebar, as the other child pedaled cautiously. When I felt that he had his balance and had developed a sense of confidence, I released the handlebar but kept my grip on the seat. My next step was to release the seat, but keep running beside the bicycle until its rider saw that he could go on without me. After that, he took off, gaily shouting over his shoulder, "Look at me!"

If more than one person assumes the task of founding a community, their ap-

Intentional Communities

---

proach must be similar: not to hold the reins too firmly, but as much as possible to involve those who come later onto the scene. The community must be seen to be theirs, as much as that of the founders.

Let us assume that the necessary initial sum has been raised. How, then, to proceed?

A good rule, based on the experience of other communities in the past, is: Don't borrow beyond a reasonable expectation of your ability to repay. Remember that the community's income will be uncertain to begin with.

At Ananda Village we were forced to borrow, but I never took a loan without personally assuming the burden of repayment — at least up to the time when I felt it was realistic to expect others to assume some, and then gradually more, of the load. It meant hard work for me, but nothing worthwhile was ever accomplished by laziness.

How to Begin

It would be wise, as I mentioned earlier, not to buy land too far away from settled areas. The community will need income, and will depend on its contacts with society at large to obtain it. It might even be wise not to settle too far away from the members' original home.

San Francisco residents, for example, would find land cheaper in Oregon than in their own area, but — assuming that they need to begin the development on a part-time basis — it would also be more difficult for them to visit Oregon regularly. Worse still, the greater distance would greatly reduce the chances of drawing new recruits from their present circle of acquaintances.

Most people would want to see the place before agreeing to live in it. Willing workers will be the community's greatest source of wealth. Why jeopardize that source by an initial saving, at the cost of continued accessibility?

If possible, land should be bought of

Intentional Communities

sufficient size to permit future expansion, or in an area which holds a promise of future land acquisition.

Although a new cooperative community will not face the hardships of a single couple starting out on their own in the woods, the standard of living will certainly not compare with that which most of the members have known in the city. The first stages of community life will have to be for people in whom the pioneering spirit is strong. Newcomers should be prepared for a life of unaccustomed simplicity.

The labor of years will bring wealth. But need an exaggerated simplicity to begin with be a burden? Surely not! For anyone who knows to its heart the bustle and complexity of big city living, a simple life can mean only welcome release from burdensome nonessentials for things more basic to one's happiness.

As much as possible of the community's initial capital should be

How to Begin

kept free for investment in various profitable ventures. The first residents may be content for some time to live in tents.

A practical, and more comfortable, alternative would be the Navajo Indian *hogan*: Secondhand beams can be bought inexpensively, arranged in a large circular pattern, narrowed slowly to form a rounded roof with an opening in the center, then covered with plastic and chicken wire, then with adobe. A movable plastic dome can be put over the opening at the top. For very little money one can have a remarkably roomy, comfortable, and well-insulated home!

Crops should be planted as early as possible. If the community is not so fortunate as to have a farming expert among its members, those in charge of the farming should have the soil tested to ascertain its quality, and get advice on how to improve it, if necessary. It would be wise to plan the crops for at least two

Intentional Communities

years ahead.

One advantage to eating one's own produce will be readily appreciated by anyone who has had a chance to dine on a farm. Really fresh fruits and vegetables are a delight simply unknown to those who must eat their food hours, or even days, after it has been picked.

It would be paradoxical for a community to embrace country life, and then to ignore the possibilities it provides for an improved diet. Almost nowhere in the cities can one find fruits and vegetables that have not been sprayed with pesticides, or treated with chemicals to make them grow larger and look better — all for the sake, not of health to the consumer, but of greater profits to the seller. Much has been written on the subject of pesticides and of chemical farming — enough, surely, to convince any thoughtful person to want his food unsprayed, and organically grown.

As insurance against future crop fail-

How to Begin

ures, the community should plan from the start to gather and store supplies of whole grain, split peas, lentils, and other non-perishable foods.

One of the most expensive, and least healthful, items in the average food budget is meat. A community will be fortunate if it can agree to be vegetarian, at least as far as its own production and official consumption are concerned (leaving room, that is, for the individual who craves meat enough to buy it for himself on the outside). Reasons for a meatless diet are given in my book, *Yoga Postures for Higher Awareness*.

A community may be surprised to discover how little money it actually requires for food. In 1950, I ate for some months on $7.50 a month, buying all my food at the grocery store. In 1960 I mentioned this feat to some friends. (They had been exclaiming on the high price of food.)

"Oh, but in 1950 everything was different!" they assured me.

Perhaps so. But in 1963 I kept a similar budget for three months. Actually, it came to $10 a month, but roughly $2.50 of this amount went for desserts and other nonessentials. All I did was omit from my diet the more expensive items: meat (which I have not eaten for most of my life), eggs, bread, butter, milk. Instead of bread, I ground my own flour and made an unleavened flat bread, like a tortilla. Frying this "chapati" (as it is called in India) in oil, I needed no butter. I trained my palate to like powered milk, which costs only a third as much as regular milk. I sprouted alfalfa seeds, ate nuts, fruits, and vegetables, made an occasional thick curried soup, or *daal*, of split peas or lentils. Raw fruits and vegetables gave me a maximum of nourishment in a minimum of bulk.

Inflation has raised the cost of everything since then. Still, one may be astonished at how well he can live on rela-

How to Begin

tively little, if he is forced to, or sufficiently motivated to try.

"The fruit of luxury," wrote Thoreau, "is luxury." The fruits of simple living, on the other hand, are peace, happiness, and freedom. For many people, it would be no deprivation at all to live without modern conveniences, perhaps with gas lights, and with wood or oil stoves, and no telephone or television!

There is a story of an American Indian who supported his family by tilling a little plot of soil less than an acre in size. He was befriended by a neighbor, a wealthy white farmer. This man, pitying his poor friend for his meager subsistence, offered him several acres of adjoining land as a gift.

"You are kind," answered the Indian. "But see: The land I have is quite enough for our needs. If I had more to till, when would I find time for singing?"

If men would only simplify their

needs, how much time might they not find to sing!

Chapter Six

Communal Economics

A vital question facing the cooperative society is that of the apportionment of wealth. The classical plan, dating as far back as apostolic days, has been for the members to own all things in common. Under this system, the individual has the use of whatever he receives from the community, but may not consider it his personal property. In monasteries, the practice has been to refer even to personal items such as sandals as "our sandals." In return for his work, the member receives everything free of charge.

Intentional Communities

In a monastic community this system has been found to work. Freedom from attachment to money and property is desirable, moreover, in one whose life is devoted to the spiritual search. Where families are concerned, I think this system is unnecessarily restrictive, and out of keeping with the consciousness of our age. It is also a real obstacle to the development of the community's economy. Even in monasteries, this practice discourages initiative, and encourages a passive dependency — questionable benefits, even in a religious calling.

The great problem with total communal ownership is that it increases the need for communal discipline. People who receive everything without paying for it must be induced somehow to work for what they get. Without the motive of personal profit, the only solution, if the community is to be productive at all, is to stress either group "spirit," or the beauty of holy obedience. Advantage is

Communal Economics

too often taken of the resident's good will. He comes for a life of peace, and in the name of group spirit finds himself launched on all sorts of glorious projects: the construction of a new library, perhaps, a hospital, a recreation center — and not just any kind of buildings, but, for the sake of the community's good name, the best imaginable.

A community I know in India, seized with this noble motive, has devoted decades to constructing a temple that — such is the dream — will be more beautiful than the Taj Mahal. To what purpose?

If people were all highly spiritual, there would be no need to regiment them to make sure they work. Nor would there be any danger lest zealous leaders regiment them so much that they *over*work. In fact, according to certain scriptures, if all people were truly spiritual they would be sustained without having to work at all. Whether or not

Intentional Communities

that will ever be the case, it is clear that we are not living at present in such a spiritual age.

It is not surprising that, in Russia, where only 3% of the cultivated land is privately owned, this tiny portion supplies fully half of all the nation's meat, milk, and green vegetables.

The early American colonies had a similar experience. Most people need to feel that they are working for themselves. They may actually be doing so just as much in a totally communistic society, but their vision is seldom broad enough clearly to grasp the fact.

Nor, it must be added, is the vision of communism's leaders any clearer. These persons tend, in most cases, to accept the worker's contribution as a matter of course, while remaining painfully conscious of the fact that, in addition to the burden of supervising his work, they must also feed, clothe, house, and entertain him. Small wonder that the benefits

Communal Economics

with which they supply him tend to be both minimal and drab. And small wonder that he is treated to harsh discipline, and told that he must obey always, and never think of himself or of his personal needs.

And if, in the case of a small intentional community, a member ever should leave, what will his recompense be? He will very likely be told that his stay there was permitted as a favor to him, that the community owes him nothing — save, perhaps, a reprimand for his ingratitude. After that, he may be given a pittance, out of "charity."

Thus it is — final indignity! — that many a monk or nun, and many a member of a completely communal society, has stayed on in the community not out of high ideals, but out of sheer economic need. In this way, he passes his latter days in frustration, infecting others with his fits of irrational temper and his jealous pride of seniority. It is a situation

Intentional Communities

comparable to that in *No Exit*, that thoroughly depressing play by Jean-Paul Sartre, the hopeless moral of which is, "Hell is other people."

No, the soundest course, it seems to me, would be to follow the pattern to which people are in any case accustomed. Let them work for wages, and in turn pay for whatever they receive. Let them save what they like for the future. "The best government," ~~Thoreau~~ [Jefferson] claimed, "is that which governs least." The simplest management in a community is as much as possible to give people the incentive to manage themselves. At Ananda Village we've always tried to keep the decision-making process at a grass-roots level. When people must look out for their own needs, they will bestir themselves well enough to produce.

There is another advantage in this method: In the usual communistic society, and in the usual homogeneous com-

Communal Economics

munity, the tendency is, as we have seen, to force people to overwork. If, however, a man must pay for everything he gets, it will be for him to decide how much income he really needs, and how many hours a week, in consequence, he must work. Under this system, if he wants to devote hours every day to painting or to meditating, he will have greater freedom to do so.

The difference between the economic system here proposed and a normal system of free enterprise is that here the member remains, as in any cooperative, a part owner of the community. Whether in higher wages, discounts, stock dividends, or special benefits, he receives his share of the community's prosperity. It is up to him, by the contribution of his labor, to increase that prosperity or to keep it lower.

Much is made in capitalistic societies of the advantages of capitalism over communism. In fact, it seems to me,

Intentional Communities

mankind is still struggling toward the ideal solution. Capitalism is certainly preferable to communism. The difference, however, is one of degree, not one of polar opposites.

Capitalism is a form of absentee landlordism. Think back to the period in France before the French Revolution. The aristocracy wanted to live luxuriously at court. They saw their properties, and the peasants working those properties, purely in the light of support for their wasteful living. The welfare of the peasants meant nothing to most of them. They rarely, if ever, saw the people from whose labor they derived their income.

Is there not a certain parallel, here, to the modern capitalistic system? Without capital no company can flourish, and this capital typically must be raised by selling shares in the company. The company's employees are not serfs in the same sense as the French peasants

Communal Economics

were. Nevertheless, those who buy stock in a company have little interest, typically, in the welfare of the workers. All they want is profits.

Wouldn't a more ideal system be one in which the workers themselves owned the company? Their interest in it would be more all-round. They would see it not only in terms of profit, but in terms of creating a pleasant working environment, products in which they could take pride, the satisfaction of being individually responsible for the growth of the company.

Such would be the benefit of living under the economic system of an intentional community.

Specifically, the system recommended here might be described as follows:

Work done for the community would be paid for, if possible, according to the member's recognized needs. Some of the community income would be earned through community-owned enterprises. The rest of it should come from a tax levied on community members and on privately owned businesses.

Private enterprise should be allowed. Enterprising members should be encouraged to form their own industries or businesses, always with the community's consent, and to employ others at wages that they can afford to pay. All members should be encouraged to contribute as much as possible *voluntarily* to the well-being of all.

To prevent anyone with sufficient wealth from controlling the community, the normal practice of cooperatives should be followed: Each member should have only one vote, regardless of how much money he puts into the community. For full voting membership, however, a person must make a minimum investment. At Ananda Village, the present membership fee is $1,500 for single persons, and $2,500 for couples.

Communal Economics

Every resident should be expected to pay monthly toward utilities, maintenance, and improvements, as well as toward taxes and any mortgage on the land.

Chapter Seven

Communalism vs. Privacy

Most spokesmen for the idea of intentional communities have made it a point to emphasize the efficiency involved in feeding and housing everyone communally. B. F. Skinner, in *Walden Two*, wrote that if it were not for such communal facilities, the community he described would be "occupying some two hundred and fifty dwelling houses and working in a hundred offices, shops, stores, and warehouses. It's an enormous simplification and a great saving of time and money."

Communalism vs. Privacy

But life offers many other satisfactions besides those that may be gleefully relished in saving time and money. I myself, when leaving the apartment I had in San Francisco on an errand, would often go out of my way to drive through Golden Gate Park. It may have been a waste in terms of time and gasoline, but the gain to my spirits made the detour worthwhile to me.

No, to say that people *must* live together for any theoretical reason would be a mistake, as indeed it would also be to say they *must* live alone. For many an individual, a house and a garden of his own epitomizes the "good life."

Granted, a completely communal life *would* be economical. Shared facilities should certainly be provided for those people who prefer them, and perhaps recommended to all. Anyone who would rather live in his own home, however, should be allowed the freedom to do so. If he wishes to eat there, too, that

Intentional Communities

should be his concern. But if, on the other hand, he prefers the ease and economy of eating with others, there is no reason why there should not be a communal dining room where he can join them.

A cohesive spirit should develop in a natural way, and not because of some theory wielded over the heads of the residents like a sledge hammer.

While members of the community should be granted a right to have homes of their own, however, newcomers might well be required to live communally for the first year. Objectionable characteristics would be more quickly observable. For the welfare of the community, only persons of reasonably harmonious disposition should be admitted to full residency.

A limit should be placed on the amount of land an individual is allowed for his private use. A person or a family who live apart should be allowed only

Communalism vs. Privacy

as much as they require for their building, with a small garden besides to protect their privacy.

In the early years at Ananda Village new members, fresh from city life, wanted to build as far from one another as possible. An abundance of land permitted a fairly wide dispersion of dwellings. In time, however, they came to the realization that they'd been isolating themselves, not from faceless strangers, but from friends, whose proximity they enjoyed.

In 1976, a devastating forest fire destroyed twenty out of twenty-one homes. In many ways, unnecessary to enumerate here, the devastation proved a blessing. From a standpoint of village planning, it enabled us to rebuild as we would have built in the first place, had we had sufficiently clear foresight.

Ananda as it was reconstructed followed a new plan of cluster housing, with the homes standing 100-150 feet from one another. Large areas of land are now open for the enjoyment of all, rather than being vaguely defined as "so-and-so's" territory simply because his home was somewhere in the vicinity.

The land should belong to the community as a whole, not to individuals. At Ananda it was found necessary, in order to avoid being classified as a condominium (the law regarding condominiums is quite strict), to keep title to the homes also in the name of the community.

Houses might all be constructed according to an accepted type. The heterogeneous impression given by so many American cities is due largely to their profusion of architectural styles. Community planning, moreover, should be directed with a view to future growth — an obvious point except for one consideration: I believe that the problem, in time, will be one of too many people rather than too few.

Communalism vs. Privacy

If the signs have been read correctly, we have entered a period in history when thousands will be drawn to this communal way of life. Paramhansa Yogananda wrote in terms of hundreds, even thousands, joining a single community. An *intentional* community of thousands, while almost certainly unacceptable to most people interested in communities today, would still be immensely preferable to the confusion of cross-currents that exists in the large cities.

An intentional community would probably elect to divide, however, long before it reached a population that was too unwieldy. One or two, or possibly a few, hundred residents might prove to be the preferred maximum. An eventual division should indeed be anticipated, and even desired, from the start. For it would be better to have many small communities in different parts of the country, where local people can visit them and benefit by observation from this new way of life, than one large community in a single place, knowable to most people only through hearsay. Better in any case a small community. Excessive size will deprive it of much of its original charm.

Let us consider, then, the case of an eventual division. For years I maintained that the ideal would be for branch communities to be autonomous. In this way, I believed, it would be possible to avoid the cumbersome system of centricity, wherein the head office sets the directions for its branches, and may feel it necessary to impose policies that are locally unsuitable.

In earlier editions of this book, I suggested "the 'colonists,' as we might call them, might be given their share out of the funds of the parent community, and perhaps also a loan without interest, and sent off on their own to found, not a branch, but another autonomous body.

Communalism vs. Privacy

For no community of this nature can be guided practically from a distance. A new community might be under the 'wing' of the parent for a time, but it must strive at the earliest possible opportunity to become independent."

As the time came for Ananda Village to start branch centers, however, it quickly became obvious that my projections were unrealistic. For one thing, the kind of members who might have been happy to go off on their own were in no case those whom we would have chosen to send, as representatives of our way of life and of our philosophy. In fact, small groups of members have elected, from time to time, to go off on their own and found communities that they envisioned as more in tune with their ideals. They have gone off with the community's blessings and good will. So far, however, none of these ventures has ever been successful.

Those members, on the other hand,

Intentional Communities

whom we considered competent to start branch centers wanted, in distancing themselves from Ananda, to affirm even more deeply their connection with the community as a whole. They didn't *want* autonomy.

A further objection to my original plan of division therefore never arose. Nevertheless it can be pointed out: How would a member's financial share in the community ever be computed? It is not like owning so many shares in a corporation. In this sense, it is not even like the worker-owned corporation I proposed earlier. Frankly, the magnitude of the problem, were it ever to arise, would very likely prove mind-boggling. At Ananda, the question has been sidestepped by placing all communal property under the ownership of a nonprofit corporation.

The problem of insensitive imposition of guidance from headquarters, one that is often encountered in corporations

Communalism vs. Privacy

with many subsidiary branches, has not arisen to date at Ananda. Here, the personal ties felt by the community with its representatives — even with those in branches as far away from California as Italy — have made collaboration exceptionally harmonious and mutually nourishing.

Even if the future should present difficulties in this regard, it seems likely at this point that a unified organization will prove preferable to a system of autonomy for each group.

Whatever the future holds, the spirit prevailing among the different communities should be the same as that which prevails among their individual members: cooperation.

Chapter Eight

Education

*"As the twig inclineth,
so doth the tree grow."*

Education plays a vital role in any community. An intentional community represents not only new opportunities for better living, but also a new outlook on life, one that can be developed most easily in childhood. If the children in the community are sent off to neighboring schools, the competitive spirit that is encouraged there will not advance their understanding of cooperation. Children are more inclined to imitate than to think

Education

things out for themselves.

The community should strive, then, as early as possible to build schools of its own — institutions where children can be taught how to *live*, not only how to add and subtract and recite from a dry catalogue of facts.

I have many friends in the teaching profession. It is surprising how many of them grumble at the public school system. Their chief complaint is that they have so little opportunity to be creative. The greater the size of an institution, the greater the need, often, for imposing uniformity on its members. Eccentricity is anathema to the established order.

In a small cooperative school, however, there would be opportunity for endless creativity. Teaching could be a constant experiment with new and better ways of imparting knowledge and understanding.

With an attractive approach to education, there is no reason why group

Intentional Communities

training, of a sort, should not begin early in life, with specially trained "baby sitters." Modern social conditioning may influence people to feel that a mother ought to be with her children all the time. But why? When she is busy with her housework she is not in any case free to play with them. They are merely in the way. The time that she can actually devote to them, once her housework has been finished, may be marred by the memory of a long day of scoldings and spankings.

My own early years were spent in Rumania, where my father worked as an oil geologist. Living there, my parents, as Americans, were able to afford a nurse. I often heard them remark that the freedom her assistance gave them made it possible for them to enjoy us much more than they would have done otherwise. And looking at the matter from our own standpoint as children, I can truthfully say that it would be difficult to imagine a happier childhood, or a greater feeling of love and respect than we felt for our parents.

Communal schooling from an early age will also help to accomplish something for which every wise parent ought to strive: expanding the child's sense of identity. The "us four and no more" attitude is not only selfish, but self-limiting. One of the best reasons for creating intentional communities is that they can help people to expand their sympathies.

To consider again my own childhood, ours was also a quasi communal life — a number of families fenced in next to a large oil refinery, named "Teleajen." Each of us gave special love to his own parents, but we addressed all the other adults affectionately as "Uncle" and "Auntie."

Why not? The community should be the child's expanded family. Thus, one may well come in time to know all men as his brothers.

Intentional Communities

It is doubtful whether competitive games and sports can be banned without washing much of the color out of a child's life. But the emphasis, certainly, should be on games in which the child can concentrate on improving his own skills rather than on beating down an opponent.

Grading, similarly, should be done as much as possible on a basis of the teacher's estimate of the child's potential rather than on a scale of comparison with other students. Comparison of one's own mental development with that of anyone else is seldom constructive. (The teacher might, however, assign an objective grade that would be kept in the student's file for future college entrance requirements, and the like.)

The children should be encouraged to develop according to each one's natural bent. Each should select, as a hobby, some special interest or trade. In this

Education

field he could receive personal training. (Every member of the community, in fact, would do well to develop some skill that could be offered for the benefit of the community.)

One of the curses of the average school system is the limits it places on creativity. It is no accident that many a creative genius has left his formal education unfinished. For the best way to receive good grades in school is to anticipate the teacher's interests. Girls generally do better than boys simply because they are often more skilled in the art of pleasing others. But the trend ought to be just the reverse: It is the teacher who should do his best to find and develop the student's interests.

The chief obstacle to the teacher's doing so, usually, is that he has a textbook to follow. As much as possible, in the community's school, teaching should be done from life itself, not from the fixed and brittle dogmas of books.

Intentional Communities

Each student should be taught also the basic arts of living: how to concentrate; the beauty of kindness and cooperation; how to overcome fear, anger, and jealousy; how to meditate and develop an inner life; how to appreciate the higher values in life. These are not matters for mere theorizing. They will require living situations and wise, personal guidance from the teachers. But they should be a vital part of any "how-to-live" school.

While teaching academic subjects, advantage should be taken of the natural tendency of children toward hero worship. They could be introduced to the lives of great men and women of history, not incidentally only, but as vitally connected with their discoveries and achievements. "A nation is known," Dr. Radhakrishnan, India's Vice President, remarked to me, "by the men and women it looks upon as great." By the same token, an emphasis on the example

Education

of certain great persons can help a child to develop clear ideals. Most children think more easily in terms of persons than of principles.

To suspend a great figure in midair, however, over the barren plains of a vanished era, would not be sufficiently instructive. That person's culture, the general interests of the people of his time, a consideration of the similarities between his age and our own — all these would help in the presentation of academic facts and principles.

In this connection, a pet educational theory of my own has long been to steep the student completely in one subject at a time, instead of obliging him to jump back and forth between completely unrelated fields: French, geometry, American history, and physics.

I remember years ago taking up a study of the fine points of English grammar. For two weeks I did nothing else. In school, a year of scattered classes and

Intentional Communities

homework assignments would have been needed to cover the same ground, and I would have forgotten most of what I had learned within a month after the final exam. Concentration it is that deepens the memory impressions in the brain. The information I absorbed in two weeks of *concentrated* study has remained with me to this day.

If a student could study one subject at a time for periods of, let us say, one month, and vary his mental fare by excursions into *related* fields, I venture to say that he would learn far more, and become far more interested in his subject in the process.

A study of algebra, for example, could involve him also in a study of the Arabs, who brought this ancient science from India. It could touch on the uses of symbolic thinking in real-life situations. It could cover the adventure of modern science, and the great scientists who brought the scientific revolution to pass.

Education

And what matter if, in the course of a year, the same subjects be touched on more than once? Approached several times in relation to different fields of interest, and therefore from different points of view, they should yield new information and wisdom every time.

I do not say that any of the above points is necessary for the development of education in an intentional community. All of them illustrate, however, an essential feature of any such education: that it be kept free for experimentation.

Chapter Nine

Government

Many utopian writers have given themselves up to dreams of a society without a government. What they have envisioned is a nation in a state of perfect equilibrium, where each person knows his own place. The old Greek, Heraclitus, had an answer for this type of thinking. "All," he said, "is flux." Living organisms achieve perfect equilibrium only in death. Otherwise, all things are in a state of movement. Death itself is only life's way of stepping aside to make way for new life forms.

Government

No, some form of government will always be necessary, and the successes and failures of countless communities suggest that it had better be a strong government. But leadership can be strong without being dictatorial. A dictatorship would be a contradiction of the spirit of a cooperative, intentional community. Granting the need for a government with the power to act as and when necessary, the best government will still be that which, as Thoreau put it, rules the least. The ideal government is one that encourages personal initiative and responsibility, and that legislates in matters of communal convenience rather than of personal outlook and growth.

The fact that man has experimented with so many different types of government suggests that the perfect system yet remains to be found. In fact, as I have already pointed out, no system can be any better than the people whose lives it directs. There can be no "perfect" system, for its members will always be the determining factor in its performance. A system can *facilitate* the expression of goodness in people; it cannot *create* goodness.

Let us, then, look for an efficient government, not a perfect one.

It would be wise for a community to seek not only efficiency, but simplicity in the management of its affairs. And the simplest form of management is supervisory, rather than authoritarian. Members, in other words, should be encouraged as much as possible to make their own decisions, always within a framework of established policy and under the general supervision of the established governing body. Members of this body might be elected annually by resident members.

My experience of life suggests that members should be eligible to vote for membership in the governing body only after they have lived in the community

Government

for at least one year. The government would be answerable to the general membership, in which the overall governing power would actually reside.

The officers would consist of a General Manager (whose position would correspond to that of the president of a corporation), a Secretary, and a Treasurer.

In addition, I recommend that there be a Spiritual Director, whose position might correspond roughly to that of Chairman of the Board.

The Spiritual Director would stand back somewhat from the day-to-day affairs of the community, in order constantly to gauge whether government and community intentions were in keeping with the community's basic philosophy. He would actively guide the community and its members toward the fulfillment of their highest ideals.

My reason for recommending a Spiritual Director is that when people are too close to a project, they often lose sight of their ideals. Or else they find themselves compromising an ideal without clearly estimating the cost involved to their first principles. Idealism, not expediency, should be the final arbiter in all community affairs. Hence the importance of not involving the Spiritual Director too directly in practical, day-to-day management. This officer's primary concern should be the community's spiritual welfare. His duty should be to coordinate the community's secular with its spiritual activities, and, by his non-involvement in secular matters, to preserve an overall view which might otherwise be lost in the exigencies of the moment.

The actual management of ongoing matters, then, would be the duty of the General Manager. He, too, should seek always to keep spiritual principles as the supreme arbiter of his activities. He should therefore be in close communica-

Government

tion with the Spiritual Director as regards the general directions taken by the governing body.

It would be counter-productive to spell out too exactly the relative powers and functions of the different officers, and particularly those of the General Manager and the Spiritual Director. The characters of the individuals in those roles will in any case be the actual determining factor in these matters.

It might be well, however, for neither the office of General Manager nor that of Spiritual Director to be a position open to a general vote by the community. The position of Spiritual Director, especially, ought, I think, to be by appointment on the part of a spiritual directorate consisting of ministers and other members with years of experience in living by the ideals of the community.

The General Manager might be appointed by the elected governing body, in consultation with the Spiritual Direc-

Intentional Communities

tor. This position, like that of Spiritual Director, is too important to the far-reaching aims of the community to be filled by a vote of the majority, many of whom, from inexperience, might not have a clear idea of the qualities required for good management. It is important, for example, that mere popularity not be a determining factor in arriving at such decisions.

On the other hand, the community's consent in all decisions is also important. In most cases, particularly when harmony prevails, that consent may be assumed. Should any group of sufficient size — say, five members — request a general referendum on any issue, however, the community should be called together and the issue put to a general vote.

It would be wise, in addition, for the community at large to be consulted on any major decisions — any proposed change of direction for the community;

Government

any decision affecting everyone for which no precedent has yet been established; any important new commitment (such as the purpose of property).

The proper balance between experience and the right of all members to be heard and properly represented can be maintained only with sensitivity and in a spirit of sincere friendship for all. Here again, no system could ever guarantee perfection. Ultimately, the smooth working of a community will depend on the spirit of its members, not on its system of government or on its bylaws.

The governing body may appoint individual members of the community to be responsible, as the need arises, for specific areas of community activity. Such positions might include the following, by way of illustration and example:

a. Director of Housing, Parks, and Community Layout
b. Director of Farming and Industrial

Planning
c. Director of Entertainment, Recreation, and Cultural Expression
d. Director of Public Relations and Instruction
e. Director of Education and Admissions
f. Director of Public Works

In order that members be selected for these posts primarily on the basis of their spiritual dedication and general executive ability, rather than on a basis of specialized knowledge in any of the above fields, members should be appointed rather than elected to these postitions. Subcommittees of specialists might be formed subsequently, under the general coordination of one or another of these Board members.

In all intentional communities, elections should be held without campaigning, and by secret ballot. Only voting members who are established residents of the community should be allowed to

Government

vote in elections of the governing body and on other "in-community" matters. Members who are not established residents might, however, be invited to offer their opinions and suggestions in many matters.

Within the framework outlined above, each member should have the same voting power as any other.

It may be necessary for new communities to grow slowly even into such a simple governmental structure as I have outlined here. For if they plunge too hastily into a cloud of formalities, they may lose sight of the real reason for which they were first drawn together.

Chapter Ten

Rules

Rules should be kept at a minimum. It is far better to establish general customs than hard and fast laws. "Too many rules," Yogananda said, "destroy an institution's spirit." Even if everyone follows a rule, the fact that it *is* a rule makes it fertile soil for gossip and suspicion. ("Did you hear that John *borrowed the garden hose* yesterday?" "Dear God, no!") It acts as a narrowing influence upon the mind, where simple customs might only help everyone to grow harmoniously. It is better, then, to deal as

Rules

much as possible with individual cases as they arise, and as circumstances dictate, without going on to establish a rule rigidly binding upon a majority who would never consider offending against it anyway.

Certain rules there will have to be, of course. It would be unfair to the newcomer to give him no clear sense of the direction in which the community is proceeding. It would also be difficult for the community to proceed smoothly toward its goals without some definite sense of what those goals were, and how best to reach them. In this respect, certainly, an intentional community must differ from the directionless hodgepodge that constitutes the average town or village.

The orientation of an intentional community should be toward the Self-realization of each of its members, and toward a spirit of cooperation. Self-realization is essentially an inward goal.

Intentional Communities

Cooperation implies a spirit that is voluntary, rather than coerced. Both ideals — personal development and group cooperation — imply a respect for one another's rights which leaves no room for egoistic individualism (the kind which carelessly imposes on the freedom of others).

Remember, too, that in an intentional community individual development and group cooperation are interactive principles. The member who sincerely seeks inner development will thereby help the others to become uplifted as well. The member, on the other hand, who makes no effort to improve himself cannot validly claim that his indolence is no one's business but his own. His laziness is a detriment to the sincere efforts of others.

Proscriptive rules should be few. One such rule should definitely take into account the fact that every community so far that has permitted the use of drugs has soon drifted into a sense of communal irresponsibility, the sure precursor to communal disintegration.

It would be wise also to prohibit alcoholic beverages as a useless indulgence among people who are trying to live a better, healthier life.

Smoking might be discouraged without any actual rule being made against it. The members might simply be asked to abstain from smoking in public places, or wherever their smoking might affect others. In all probability the very concept of an intentional community will minimize this problem, if it doesn't eliminate it altogether. The best solution, then, may be not to treat it as a problem.

At Ananda, where most of the members are vegetarian, the question of meat-eating also is treated in this way.

Here are a few suggestions, only, for basic rules that a community might do well to adopt:

Intentional Communities

1. No job shall be played up as more dignified than any other.

2. No one may act in such a way as to harm another. (This rule might be interpreted subtly, as well as literally, for a negative personal example can, in certain cases, be as injurious to a community as actual physical violence.)

3. Voting must be considered a right, but also a privilege, rather than a duty. No one should vote unless he has formed a definite opinion on the subject under consideration.

4. No hallucinogenic drugs or alcoholic beverages may be taken by any member of the community, on or off the community property.

Chapter Eleven

What is Ananda?

The reader has already been informed that an actual experiment in cooperative living, known as Ananda World Brotherhood Village, is being carried out by the author and some of his friends in the mountains of northern California on the basis of the ideas presented in this book. You may yourself have wondered more than once already, "Why go to all the trouble of starting something myself, when there is a community already flourishing that I might join?"

Intentional Communities

As a matter of fact, we might be happy if you reached this conclusion. But please bear in mind that communities, like people, develop distinct characters of their own. To live in a place with a different character from yours might impede your development, even though its essential goals and yours be the same. Many are the roads to truth, and many and varied are the possible applications of broad principles, such as those which have been outlined in these pages.

Ananda presents one such application. Not everyone who reads this book and is attracted by its ideas will necessarily feel attracted to the community I have founded. This is, I believe, quite as it should be. The world would be a very dull place if everyone liked and did all the same things. The most universal principles must lose some of their universality on actual application, for every such application can only be a limited *example* of the principles themselves.

What is Ananda?

Other, and perhaps very different, applications might exemplify the principles just as truly.

Information on Ananda World Brotherhood Village may be obtained by visiting or writing to us. It may also be obtained in considerable detail by reading my book, *Cities of Light*.

Ananda was founded during a two-year period, from 1967-69. Since then it has grown and flourished to become one of the most successful intentional communities anywhere.

Ananda is not sectarian in its dealings with the general public. We find it helpful, however, in our own home environment for our members to be following the same path together.

And what is this path? A few of its highlights may be expressed thus:

A belief in the essential oneness of all religions, and a universal respect for their teachings.

A belief in the value of meditation,

and in the spiritual life as the summum bonum of human existence.

Respect for the great saints of all religions, who have fulfilled in their own lives the highest spiritual teachings.

A belief that it is insufficient merely to believe — that spiritual truths must be practiced and *experienced* in one's own life, through meditation.

The fact that Ananda exists, and that it has achieved a remarkable degree of success, should give hope to others who would like to found similar communities, but who fear that after all the whole idea, in this age of business mergers and sprawling urban communities, might prove impracticable.

Some people would rather join an already-working venture. Others would prefer the challenge of starting such a venture themselves. If you yourself fit into either of these categories, I hope that this book will help you to determine a life direction that might make all the difference between a richly meaningful life and one that lacks clear direction.

If this book succeeds in this aim, I will feel myself amply rewarded.

Epilogue

If you would like to write or phone to Ananda World Brotherhood Village for further information about the community, or about guest programs designed to give one experience of the community, you may do so at:

14618 Tyler Foote Road
Nevada City, California 95959
(916)292-3065

For further study on related subjects, I would recommend the following of my books:

Cities of Light describes Ananda as it has developed over the years, and explores more deeply the relevance of these communitarian ideals to modern society.

The Art of Supportive Leadership gives helpful guidelines to the kind of leadership that is particularly important for the formation of intentional communities.

Education for Life (or, as the title is going to be changed to read: *Growing Up — Learning to Relate to Others' Realities*) goes deeply into the question of education of children. This book is particularly helpful for people living in intentional communities.

Crises in Modern Thought — Solutions to the Problem of Meaninglessness. This book addresses problems raised by the discoveries of modern science, and the impact of those discoveries on traditional values.

A Selection of Other Books by J. Donald Walters

Cities of Light — What Communities Can Accomplish, and the Need for Them in Our Times.

Crises in Modern Thought — Solutions to the Problem of Meaninglessness.

The Artist as a Channel — a book that proposes a new approach to the Arts, one that combines deep, intuitive feeling with clear and meaningful insight.

The Search — A Young Person's Quest for Understanding. This autobiography is a deeply moving revelation of a poignant search for truth.

Rays of the Same Light (3 Volumes) — Parallel Passages, with Commentary, from the Bible and the Bhagavad Gita.

The Art of Supportive Leadership — a practical handbook for people in positions of responsibility.

Education for Life — a book on childhood education (to be renamed **Growing Up** — **Learning to Relate to Others' Realities**).

How To Be a Channel — how to truly transmit inspiration received from sources other than the ego.

Affirmations & Prayers — a collection of 52 spiritual qualities and a discussion of each, with an affirmation and prayer for its realization.

"Secrets" series — daily thoughts for the month:

Secrets of Happiness

Secrets of Success

Secrets of Attracting and Keeping Friends

Secrets of Persuasion

Secrets of Meditation

Secrets of Inner Peace

Secrets of Overcoming Harmful Emotions